Zoom In on
Savanna Animals

Elephants

Leo Statts

abdopublishing.com

Published by Abdo Zoom™, PO Box 398166, Minneapolis, Minnesota 55439. Copyright © 2017 by Abdo Consulting Group, Inc. International copyrights reserved in all countries. No part of this book may be reproduced in any form without written permission from the publisher. Abdo Zoom™ is a trademark and logo of Abdo Consulting Group, Inc.

Printed in the United States of America, North Mankato, Minnesota
062016
092016

THIS BOOK CONTAINS RECYCLED MATERIALS

Cover Photo: Claudia Paulussen/Shutterstock Images
Interior Photos: Shutterstock Images, 1; Britta Kasholm-Tengve, 4–5; Mike Dexter/Shutterstock Images, 6; William Davies/iStockphoto, 7; John Michael Evan Potter/Shutterstock Images, 8, 10; Jiri Foltyn/iStockphoto, 9; Andrey Kuzmin/iStockphoto, 11; iStockphoto, 12–13, 16; Red Line Editorial, 13, 20 (left), 20 (right), 21 (left), 21 (right); Johan Swanepoel/iStockphoto, 14; Lauren Case/iStockphoto, 15; Jay Hendry/iStockphoto, 17; Angelika Stern/iStockphoto, 18–19; Francois Van Heerden/iStockphoto, 19

Editor: Emily Temple
Series Designer: Madeline Berger
Art Direction: Dorothy Toth

Publisher's Cataloging-in-Publication Data
Names: Statts, Leo, author.
Title: Elephants / by Leo Statts.
Description: Minneapolis, MN : Abdo Zoom, [2017] | Series: Savanna animals | Includes bibliographical references and index.
Identifiers: LCCN 2016941163 | ISBN 9781680792003 (lib. bdg.) | ISBN 9781680793680 (ebook) | ISBN 9781680794571 (Read-to-me ebook)
Subjects: LCSH: Elephants--Juvenile literature.
Classification: DDC 599.67--dc23
LC record available at http://lccn.loc.gov/2016941163

Table of Contents

Elephants 4

Body 8

Habitat 12

Food 14

Life Cycle 16

Quick Stats. 20

Glossary 22

Booklinks 23

Index 24

Elephants

Elephants are large **mammals**.

They are kind.
They care for one another.

If one elephant is hurt,
the others move slowly.

This allows the hurt elephant to keep up.

Body

Elephants have thick, gray skin.

An elephant has a long nose.
It is called a trunk.

Elephants have big ears.
The ears are floppy.

Most elephants have **tusks**.

Habitat

Most wild elephants live in Africa. Some live in Asia. Elephants can be found in **savannas**. They also live in **tropical** forests.

■ Where elephants live

Food

Elephants need a lot of food. They eat grasses and fruits.

Roots and bark are common, too. They use their trunks to eat.

Life Cycle

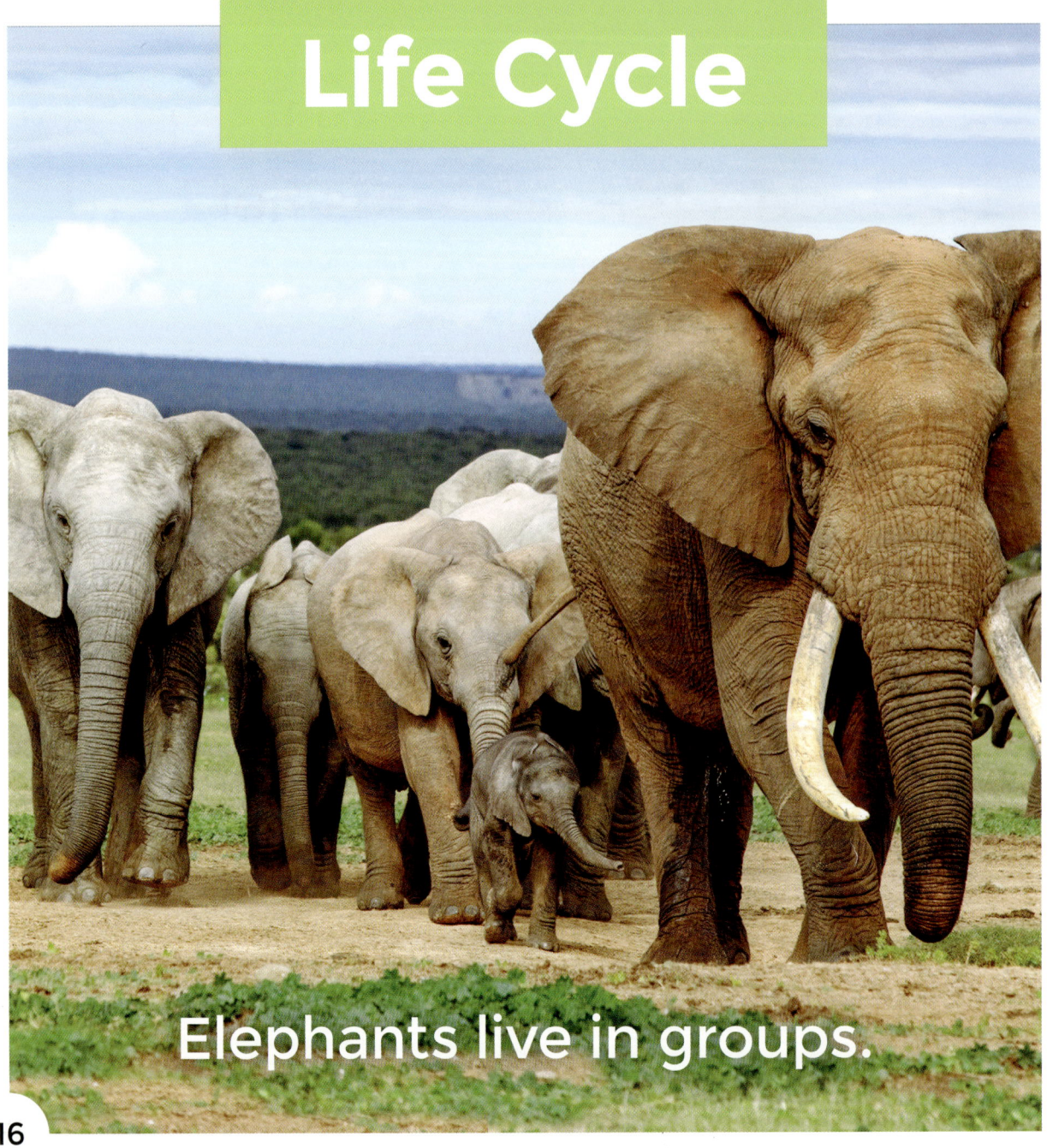

Elephants live in groups.

The groups are called herds.
The oldest female leads her herd.

Elephants usually have one baby.
They can live for 50 years.

Average Height

An elephant is as tall as a basketball hoop.

10 ft   10 ft

Average Weight

A baby elephant weighs almost as much as a refrigerator.

187 lbs   200 lbs

Glossary

mammal - an animal that makes milk to feed its young and usually has hair or fur.

root - the part of a plant that grows underground.

savanna - a grassland with few or no trees.

tropical - weather that is warm and wet.

tusks – long teeth that stick out of an animal's mouth.

Booklinks

For more information on **elephants**, please visit booklinks.abdopublishing.com

 **In on Animals!**

Learn even more with the Abdo Zoom Animals database. Check out **abdozoom.com** for more information.

Index

baby, 19

ears, 10

eat, 14, 15

groups, 16, 17

hurt, 6, 7

kind, 5

live, 12, 13, 16, 19

nose, 9

skin, 8

trunk, 9, 15

tusks, 11